Through My Eyes

To a
Good Human
[signature]

Through My Eyes

By
Chief James R. Sherbaugh, Jr.

E-BookTime, LLC
Montgomery, Alabama

Through My Eyes

Library of Congress Control Number: 2008909229

ISBN: 978-1-59824-937-8

First Edition
Published October 2008
E-BookTime, LLC
6598 Pumpkin Road
Montgomery, AL 36108
www.e-booktime.com

Contents

Introduction

The best way for me to help you understand what is in this book is for you to listen and look. That's right, read some of it, then refer to what is in the King James Bible, and if you can, Greek mythologies and Mohawk visions and dreams. Then take all the information that you have gathered in your brain and turn off the television, stereo, phone, and any other noise making devises.

Now you will be able to look at your thoughts on what you have read. One at a time, look at each thought. One at a time, look to see what it is showing you, look at the action; look at the beginning to the end, then the final outcome. You must first try to separate your thoughts from your body and your mind to do this. Your mind is full of clutter and things that you think you need and crave for your body; worries, doubt, anger, and so on. Your body is not you, that is right. It is what you, the real you, lives in at the moment. The conscience is you; the small, quiet voice that sometimes lets you know that this is wrong, or yes, this is the right thing to do. You feel it. You know it from your heart, not the mind. Listening to the mind feels so good, but stop. That's not what you are to listen to.

Your spirit and The Holy Spirit in you is what I am trying to help you get in touch with. Ah yes, that's right, you are a Christian. You don't believe this or you think that you are already doing this. Maybe you are or maybe you're not. Make sure. Go ahead, because you may be deceived, that you think it is The Holy Spirit, but it's not; it is your brain. It is the thoughts and suggestions from outside the temptations that we let run our lives like anger, greed, and so on.

This will take a few attempts I am sure of it, but when you get it, you will know because you will actually see the processes, but at first, it may be a little hard. Then it will become easier and comforting. The real truth will be given to you. You see, we have been lied to and brainwashed to think in one level only; on this earth, and as everyone else, the easy way; the things of this world, and only what you can see, and if it is not true, it is then dismissed.

Reality to man is what he perceives it to be, but that is not always the truth. The truth is within you. It is a gift. All you have to do is ask for it, and then truly be willing to accept it. Not put our truth to it. This is what to look for. Your truth can be convenient, compromised, and instant satisfaction of the physical need. The holy truth is to act in such a way that you are living forever. This is very hard, but can be done. Just remember, there are other worlds; this is the physical, and also the spiritual. There is only a fine line that separates them, one behind the other, or below and above one another, in spiritual word estates or spires, and there is a war against the Saints. It started back with Adam and Eve and is continuing this day. This is the truth.

The Vision

It all started to become clear in the year of 1993. Back in the summer of 1993, I was in a small truck stop for the night, at Hurricane, WV. It was very hot, so I was sitting in the cab with the door open on the cab of the truck. Then, out of nowhere, a small-built old man came from the wood line. The old man walked straight over to my truck and said to me, "I have something to tell you." He had gray, short hair, with wrinkled skin. The old man looked healthy for his age, wearing a red hanky as a sweat band, cowboy boots and jeans with a blue jean jacket. The old man was soft spoken, but firm.

He said, "You are a Native, you know, Indian, and so am I." Then as the old man looked at the earth, he said, "I am a drunk, as many of us have become. Don't become like this."

Then a long pause. Then the old man said, "I am also on the run from the law in Colorado for drunken disorder. It all started in Flagstaff, Arizona. The US Government was rounding up the wild mustangs into a boxed cannon. Then, the soldiers would start shooting most of them. They then took a dozen or so to the reservations. The wild mustangs, most of the time, were sick and had worms. The soldiers wouldn't let the Indians have any of the good horses. "I tried to protest," the old man said sadly, "what I was seeing, but was thrown in jail for being a drunk. Then they, the government, sent me to Colorado. That is when I had gotten away. They, the US Government, are looking for me."

Then the old man slowly pulls an old yellow piece of paper out of his blue jean jacket and hands it to me. The paper was a warrant for his arrest, from the state of Colorado, dated 1864. I handed it back to him and said, "I guess you'd better be going."

The old man said, "Soon, but first I have to say to you. Don't forget or hide who you are. Our people need help with things that will

14

happen. You will see things that can help. You will become a leader, and you will fall very ill, but live long, don't forget. I must go." He then turned and walked away. As the old man walked away he was also fading away.

It was in the early part of summer in 1996 when I saw the layout of what was to come. I wanted to do a sweat in my back yard, but didn't have time to get things set up properly. I decided to go up stairs and run a very hot cast iron tub of water. It was mostly hot water filled almost to the limit and too hot to touch. I sat next to the cast iron tub for a short time in prayer.

The small room was hazed up at this time, to the point of one and a half foot of visibility at most. By now, I can just touch the water, not worrying about getting burned. I quickly slid into the piping hot water up to my shoulders. Having most of my body under water as possible in a short time, I got light-headed. I hadn't had any food for thirty-eight hours, so that came into play. I was also very groggy. Soon it got very quiet and still. This is what I was hoping for.

Still, as if nothing else going on in the world matters, it just stops. Yes stops; sound, movement; the world stops. All of a sudden the haziness is gone and I see two men sitting on the ground in front of a fire across from each other in the evening night; two men dressed in old native clothing. The older man on the left was wearing white. He was a small man five feet four, at most, and slightly bent over his hair is all gray. The shirt that he wore was long-sleeved and had tassels under the arms all the way down to his hands that held a pipe in them; the shirt and pants both made of cotton and white. The pants seemed to be a type of lagans; other than that, very plain and simple. The younger man was dressed in a plain, buck skin, long sleeve shirt and plain long pants.

At once, the young man got up from the ground and started to run as fast as he could. I think he was running north. All of a sudden, something was chasing behind him about one hundred yards, and closing quickly. As it got closer, I could see it clearly; a wolf, a white wolf. In no time, the wolf had caught up to the young man and jumped into the man.

Then the man shape shifted into a white wolf as he was running, and then back into a man again, and then back to a wolf. The wolf ran back to the old man and sat down across from him on the ground in front of the fire. As the old man began to talk to the wolf, it began to fade as the fire was reflecting off of the image. Then the young man appeared with the wolf sitting beside him. The old man continued with his instructions as if nothing had happened. The old man reached down beside him and picked up the staff that was on the ground and handed it to the young man. Then the old man sent smoke to the Creator and passed the pipe over to the young man. The young man sent smoke to the Creator also, and then passed the pipe to the wolf, and then he did the same.

After every one was content, the pipe went back to the old man. Then the young man and the wolf got up and were walking away. The young man's clothes changed to cotton and became white. The cane that he now has was

less than three foot in length and light in color
and was twisted.

Later, I see the same young man in all white
standing on a stage in front of a crowd of
people wearing all white, and of all races, as
far as you can see, made up the multitude. As
everyone was looking up, the man raised his
cane up and out to the crowd parallel to the
ground.

The cane began to fill up rapidly with the
bluest of blue water, as the cane had become
transparent. After a few seconds, the cane
turned to crystal, then everything stops; the
vision is over. The young man was trying to
run away from his ancestors and from who he
is. The old man, an old spirit, needed to speak
to the young man in the spirit world; to show
him the gifts that he has waiting for him; the
knowledge.

The spiritual gifts are for him to use as tools
the Creator has available for the young man to
use. Don't be mistaken, the old man is not the
Creator, but a messenger for the Creator. You
could say an angel because they are God's

messenger. The white wolf was sent out to retrieve the young man. The young man has wolf clan in his nation; they are his cousins.

The Native American families are broken down into clans. Each clan is represented by an animal, bird, or fish. The clans followed the mother's side, not the father. And the people of a clan usually had some of the behaviors of the animal or bird, or so on, that represented what clan they belonged to.

Some clans had special gifts. For example, if you are from the bear clan, you will have a greater chance of being a healer of some type. One of the primary reasons the Indian was given clans was to ensure that no inbreeding could take place. If you are a man from the turtle clan you were not permitted to take a woman from that clan as a wife. So when a turtle clan man, for example, marries a woman from the bear clan, the children are to be of the bear clan. I think this was stopped on the reservations around 1868 by the United States Government. And I do know, in 1924 at Buffalo Creek [Buffalo, NY.], the Federal Government launched a major campaign against this, and it was a major blow to the Native Americans. The clan was the center, the nucleus, of everything to the Indians. Most of the ceremonies are built around the clans. The rules of Government and positions in council were even dictated by your clan.

Even where you could set in the council meeting depended on your clan. Almost everything that was to be, or is to be, revolved around clans, the family unit. It was the fabric of the family which made up the nations. Clans were how you operated, from the smallest things in life as an individual, and up to the actions and behavior patterns of the nation and their Government. You see, a long time ago no one really knows how long ago, some say thousands of years, the natives had no stable government that followed the laws of one Creator. There were no morals as you could imagine; a lot of murder and cannibalism. Then a man came from the west and traveled to the east with a message of peace, power, and righteousness. The Mohawk Nation was the first to accept this law. It is called the Great Law. The man who brought this to them was called the Peace Maker. This was the same man that gave the grandmothers the clan system. I think this man may have been Jesus Christ who came to save all people.

So the white wolf was also a messenger of the spirit. Shape shifting is done in the spiritual world all the time. Angel means "messenger", and can also be a protector. The young man accepted the messenger and the responsibilities and duties of the creator, then the white wolf, the angel, for say, was sent or delivered to the man to protect him against all evil doers. The white wolf's name is Spirit, and she has brown eyes that beam a very white intense light from them. The cane was delivered to the young man first. The cane is to be used as a very powerful spiritual tool of symbolism. The cane will represent many different groups of people. When the people are reborn of the spirit, through the water with which gives them life, they will become strong and stable, and as clear as crystal they will see.

God gave Moses a staff to use as a great tool so that he may set the Jews free from the Pharaoh. **[Exodus 7: 10]** And Moses and Aaron went in unto Pharaoh, and they did so the Lord had commanded, and Aaron cast down his rod before Pharaoh, and before his servants, and it became a serpent. Now the cane is there, and the white wolf has been delivered. The message is being delivered. All there is left is for the people to put down their idols of this world and to praise God, the only father, and you will be delivered to God by Jesus and will receive the gift of eternal life. The old man would also be an angel giving me the information that is needed. In native culture, the wise old man is called old man out of respect. You are to lessen and learn from him. To call him anything less than old man is to insult him. When around a fire with old people, it is rude to cross between the two. The Chief or oldest is to always face to the east. When you are finished with an issue, a pipe is passed filled with pure tobacco. If you do not smoke from it, you are not being true. When you send up smoke from the pipe, you send your prayers and praises to the Creator.

In ceremony, you can put sage, tobacco, and berry leaves. This also entails a special pipe. It must have a round bowl to represent mother earth. The bowl must receive the stem. The stem must come apart into three parts. There should be some fur or antler, or hide to represent the animals. I also like to have some bird feathers to show their representation. We used a personal pipe. They are much smaller around pocket size and one piece. It is good for one or two people. A modest man is more content with such a pipe if he can get away with it. But it is limited in its use.

Angels And Demons

When people think of Angels, they think of nice little babies with wings or beautiful woman, but never Satan in the same sentence. No sin; not even a blemish. That was the intent of the Creator.

But it doesn't always work out that way. Chances are your church windows shows Angels in a very stereo type. Unfortunately, you have been mislead and you have missed out on so much more. We are going to start from the beginning, Genesis, and work our way to Revelations on real angel and demons. We will discover the different types of Angels, and why and what happened, and that they are sons of God. **[Gen 6: 1-4] 1** *And it came to pass, when men began to multiply the face of the earth, and daughters were born unto them,* **2** *That the sons of God saw the daughters of* *men that they were fair; and they took them wives of all which they chose. 3 And the Lord said "my spirit shall not always strive with man, for that he also is flesh: yet his days shall be an hundred and twenty years." 4 There were giants in the earth in those days; and also after that, when the sons of God came in unto the daughters of men, and they bare children to them, the same became mighty men which were of old, men of renown.* **[Job 1:6]** *Now there was a day when the sons of God came to present themselves before the Lord, and Satan came also among them.* **[Job 2:1]** *Again there was a day when the sons of God came to present themselves before the Lord, and Satan came also among them to present himself before the Lord.* **[Job 38:4-7]** *4 Where was thou when I laid the foundations of the earth? Declare, if thou hast understanding. 5 Who hath laid the measures thereof, if thou knowest? Or who hath stretched the line upon it? 6 Whereupon are the foundations thereof fastened? Or who laid the corner stone thereof; 7 when the morning stars sang together, and all the sons of God shouted for joy?*

In the beginning God made Angels without sin and with male gender as God still does today. God has many different types of angels. Their main job is to be a messenger for God. Though they do often get assigned other jobs, Angels are spirit beings that have great powers. They can look almost like any living creature they choose. Angels in their normal bodies are larger than man and are the most handsome of men. At the same time, they have a slight female look. Angels can eat food, but they don't need to. They don't even need sleep; angels can make themselves large and small. Angels can blow winds like a hurricane. They can make great battles on nations. Angles have many more great powers beyond man. Angels don't bleed. They don't feel pain like you and I. God assigns angels to stars and planets. Right now angels are allowed to protect you from physical and spiritual things, but there are rules and limitations set by God. **[Jude vs. 9]** *Yet Michael the archangel, when contending with the devil he disputed about the body of Moses, durst not bring against him a railing accusation, but said, The Lord, "rebuke thee."*

Angels are not to take away your free will at any time. They can only make a suggestion to you or nudge you in most instances. Angels are capable of sin. They cannot reproduce among their own. But Angels can physically mate with our women. God forbids such acts, for they are out of their natural dimension and are in sin when they fornicate in this manner. And these angels have fallen from grace and are resaved in everlasting chains under darkness unto judgment day, in their attempt to pollute the human stock. An example is in **[Jude vs7]**. *Even as Sodom and Gomorrah, and the cities about them in like manner, giving themselves over to fornication, and going after strange flesh, set forth an example, suffering the vengeance of eternal fire.*

There was an angel that God had made the most beautiful creature of all his creations. This angel was on the right hand of God, and his name was Lucifer. This angel, Lucifer, was the biggest and most powerful of them all. But that wasn't enough for Lucifer. And he convinced one-third of the holy angels to rebel. They did with Lucifer against God our father. So God sent them all to hell

27

[Revelations 12:3] *And there appeared another wonder in heaven; and behold a great red dragon, having seven heads and ten horns, and seven crowns upon his heads.*
[Revelations 12 7-12] *7 And there was a war in heaven: Micheal and his angels fought against the dragon; and the dragon fought and his angels. 8 And prevailed not; neither was their place found any more in heaven. 9 And the great dragon was cast out, that old serpent, called the Devil, and Satan, which deceiveth the whole world: he was cast out into the earth, and his angels were cast out with him. 10 And I heard a loud voice saying in heaven, Now is come salvation, and strength, and the kingdom of our God, and the power of his Christ: for the accuser of our brethren is cast down, which accused them before our God day and night. 11 And they overcame him by the blood of the lamb and by the word of their testimony; and they loved not their lives unto the death. 12 Therefore, rejoice, ye heavens, and ye that dwell in them. Woe to the inhabiters of the earth and of the sea! For the devil is come down unto you, having great wrath, because he knoweth that he hath but a short time. Many of them had sin*

of fornication, **[2nd Pet 2:4]** *For God spared not the angels that sinned, but cast them down to hell. And delivered them into chains of darkness, to be reserved unto judgment;* **[Jude 6-7]** *And the angels which kept not their first estate, but left their own habitation, he hath reserved in everlasting chains under darkness unto the judgment of the great day. 7 Even as Sodom and Gomorrah, and the cities about them in like manner, giving themselves over to fornication, and going after strange flesh, are set forth for an example, suffering the vengeance of eternal fire.*

When the angels mated with human women, this made a half breed and a very abnormal human with power that we don't have. And I think that was the birth of Greek mythology. These are ungodly men of great power, and to some would look like gods. Let's get a good example of a good angel, Micheal, an Archangel. Did you know that Micheal fought with the devil for Moses' body until Christ conquered the devil on the Cross? Then God took Moses body and buried it in Moah. This is in **[Jude vs. 9]**.

So far we have covered common angels, arch angels, and fallen angels that chose to sin. Now let's get into the demons, the unclean spirits. There are many different types, but they all have one thing in common; to work in the physical world they must use a host. The host can be a person or an animal; any living thing can be used. You probably can't see them, but you can't see the wind, only the effects, when a mother of a crying baby allows herself to get so angry at the baby that she picks the baby up and shakes it to death.

Ok, you might not see that one. A woman has been seen for severe depression and is placed on medication to help her. The world looks so unsafe for her little baby that she is unable to protect them in her mind. Then, one morning the woman hears a voice in her head. You must undo what you have done. You have brought these poor little helpless children into this dangerous world, for them only to suffer. There is only one way for you to save them. Yes, only you can save them. You must cut them up into little pieces so that no one can find them, and then they will be safe. Then she hears the voice over and over again. No one is looking at her spirit. They are only trying to control her mind.

Finally, the woman makes her choice to take her babies out of this world as she has been instructed to do so that no one or nothing can find them. It is possible to see them sometimes. I have seen some of them myself. Sometimes I can hear them, and more often than not, I have learned how to hear them and or recognize them. It is a touchy thing. It is a matter of slowing your thoughts and/or the ones around you. You must, truly in your mind, separate your mind from your body, as you are in spirit. Then, stand apart from them and look at your thoughts. Try and see where they are leading you.

To do this, you must not be of this world. Only then can you truly see the demons clearly. We all have them at some level. This is why it is so important to allow Christ into your heart so that you don't become controlled by unclean spirits. Some demons when separated from the host may be seen. The unclean spirits when commanded out of a host with the authority of Christ will cause a man to have seizures as they are being removed. Demons are disembodied spirits, that, on their own, cannot physically operate in this dimension. So they must jump from body to body. But I have seen some in the middle, and this is not to happen.

As end times are getting closer and closer, it seems to me that the rules are getting bent. Some are tall and dark like darkness that you have never seen, and have long arms, long legs and slender bodies. Remember, they're not to have their own body. They have round heads and a lot of sharply pointed teeth. Almost like a man crossed with a monkey without a tail. Some are more animal-like, but mixed up and very dark. Others only look to be a never ending black mark. Demons like to work in groups for they are cowards. For example: a person with multiple personalities. Demons are allowed to control or suppress man and beast that have week minds, and spirits. **[St. Mark 5: 13]** *And forthwith Jesus gave them leave. And the unclean spirits went out, and entered into the swine: and the herd ran violently down a steep place into the sea, (they were about two thousand;) and were* *choked in the sea.* They also love to tempt the Godly man even more just as Satan did Jesus. **[St. Matthew 4:8]** *Again, the devil taketh him up into an exceeding high mountain, and showeth him all the kingdoms of the world, and the glory of them; 9 And saith unto him, all these things will I give thee, if thou wilt fall down and worship me.*

Demons are not to be trusted. They will work through your emotions, hate, fear, anger, self-pity, pride, and so on. They will try to reason with you with half truths. They will build on your insecurities. Demons live through you if you let them. This is where free will comes into play. We are always being approached by unclean spirits of this world, all day all night. Yes, they are worse than a telemarketer. But just remember they have to have permission. You can give it conscious or unconscious, it's all the same. **[St. Matthew 10:8]** *Heal the sick, cleanse the lepers, raise the dead, cast out the devils; freely ye have received, freely give.*

Unclean spirits also have to answer to Jesus Christ. A demon will see Christ as the son of

God and must fallow his commands. **[St. Mark 16:17]** *And these signs shall follow them that believe in my name shall they cast out devils; they shall speak with new tongues.* Demons are condemned to hell. When the final judgment time comes, they have no other place to go. There are levels to hell as there are in heaven. There is a level of hell here on earth in some places, just as there is a level of heaven that can be seen, heard, smelled, or felt in some cases. You can live forever, or you can die forever. It is up to you.

The first Sunday in September 2005, my wife and I was attending church in a small town that we haven't been to in some time. The church has a small congregation, and is suffering, spiritually, and financially. A young teenage boy, that my wife and I know, always greets us, and he had sat beside me this day. He is on medication for A.D.D. He has the fidgeting that comes and goes. But today was different. The truth was about to be shown. The boy was moaning and groaning under his breath. Then he was rocking more and more. By the time the minister was giving the sermon, the boy was starting to show that he was possessed by a demon.

I started to pray for the boy in Jesus' name. The boy started rocking faster and faster. Then he would look at me as to dare me. Then he started talking in tongues. The boy finally got loud enough that some of the other people around us could hear him. My wife could hear him growling. I then placed my left hand on the base of his neck. We were standing at that time. I then demanded that the demon leave the boy, and be cast to Hell in the name of Jesus Christ. The boy fell to the chair in front of him. He was hanging onto the back of the chair and trying to hide his face at the same time. My wife said his face was getting pushed out of shape with his hands. She said he had a lot of skin around his eyes. Then it stopped; all movement; all space and time.

A soft voice came to me from inside and not in words. He said, "Not now. This is a done deal." So I moved my hand from the boy's left shoulder. He, the boy, then slowly got back to his feet in a dazed kind of way. A few seconds later, the boy turned and ran out of the church! I didn't see the boy for the rest of the day.

Now we are going to talk about demons and angels in the mind when you dream. The Mohawks believe that dreams are very important in the physical world as well as the spirit world; that they are a window for you to look into the spirit world, and that if you don't play act out in the physical world, they will happen anyways. This could be bad or good, so if it is something bad like murder, they would play act it out under the supervision of a spiritual leader in hopes that it, the demons, won't manifest it in the physical world. The Bible also gives you examples of spiritual windows in this dream world.

Also, the dreams can be an extension of what happened in the physical world by showing you the behind the scenes in spirit form. This next story is a good example of this, and it is a true story. The dream was in black and white picture form and clear. In the evening, the lady said she was standing on a hill top looking down onto a cemetery and on the cemetery was a carnival. On the far side of the cemetery, the lady said that in the dream, she walked down the side of the hill, then, she cut through the cemetery to the far side, with the hill to her back. When she got to the first carnival tent, she said she lifted the flap and went inside.

When inside, there were a lot of people. As she moved around through the tent, she noticed that all the faces were unfamiliar to her. It seemed that she was looking for someone or something. When the woman came to realize that the people that she was looking for wasn't in the tent, she left the tent on the other side. When she was outside, in a short distance, she noticed another top tent. So she walked over to the tent and went inside. It seemed to be of no real surprise that she had found the group of people that she knew and had been looking for, mixed with the other people that she didn't know. The people that she was looking for were family members in one capacity or another.

The lady made herself known to the family members in question. When she had gotten their attention, she said that she put her hand into her chest, and pulled it out with great pain. The object that she pulled out was a man's head covered in blood. That's right, she had pulled a man's severed head out of her chest by the hair, and then held it up for everyone to see, especially for the ones that she knew. As the lady was holding up the severed head in the crowd, she said, "You see, I killed it, and I have the power to bring it back to life if I so choose to do so!" The lady then put the disembodied head on a lance for all to see. Then the lady said she woke up, and her chest hurt for about a week, and that's all she can remember.

This dream was a very important spiritual event for the woman and the reasons are more complicated than the dream. I am going to do my best to help you understand. When this lady was a young girl, she was unfortunately molested by at least one of the family members physically. She had no one to turn to for help. When the young girl had tried to confide in other close family members, she was denied help in any shape, way, or form. This is sadly too common in America today. We tend to put our personal wants before our children's needs when it comes down to it, with some people. So the little girl continued to be destroyed by the demons in her family for a lengthy period of time. The emotional and spiritual damage is devastating, and now the lady was being tortured on a daily basis non stop.

The dream was a battle against the demons of her family members that so willingly robbed her of life by this act and other acts of uncleanliness. As the lady had become an adult and sought out God, she was given the power to go into the spirit world and confront the demons that had imposed their unclean will onto a child, and battles in the spirit world are just as painful, if not more than in the physical world.

Animals Can Be Possessed Also

A lot of people think that animals don't have a soul and can't be possessed, and others think everything and everyone is possessed. I don't understand how they come to that conclusion. It's really funny when someone says the Bible tells them this. I think they better read the King James Bible again before they say such ignorant things. When I am done with this story, I will have shown you the real facts as I understand them to be. Keep in mind, just because you don't understand it, that does not mean that it isn't. Just because you can't see something that does not mean that it isn't there. Here is a good example. You can't see the wind, but you know it's there. You see the effect that it makes on things around you if you look and listen. Just like the spirit world, you may not be able to see it, but it has an effect on life around you all the time. Just keep that tucked in the back of your mind and I will get on with these true events.

When I was a young boy growing up in south western Pennsylvania, I did some trapping. I wasn't allowed to have a gun, not even a BB gun. Later, I got smarter after trying to club a possum to death, and drown a raccoon. The only one beat was me, with some very mad animals on my hands. If you had asked me at that moment if they were possessed, I would have mistakenly said yes! Later, I learned to use a ball bat in such a way that I could snap the neck very fast.

There was one raccoon with only three legs and as big as a coyote. He liked to make me think he was possessed. Almost every morning he would see me walking up the road, so he would walk out into the middle and stop to growl at me, but he always let me pass after he had a good laugh. He was just a jerk. He was like some people I know. And no, most people are not possessed either; they just want you to be miserable, as did the raccoon. If I am miserable, you have to be too; this is how that works. It is not often that you will find an animal or animals possessed. When you do, you better know what you are doing because animals are possessed in groups, or the demons in one will jump to another animal. Let's look at the King James **Saint Mark Ch. 1 vs. 23 thru 26, 34**

- **23** *And there was in their synagogue a man with an unclean spirit; and he cried out,*
- **24** *Saying let us alone; what have we to do with thee, thou Jesus of Nazareth? Art thou come to destroy us? I know thee who thou art, the Holy One of God.*
- **25** *And Jesus rebuked him, saying,* **Hold thy peace, and come out of him.**
- **26** *and when the unclean spirit had torn him, and cried with a loud voice. He came out of him.*
- **34** *And he healed many that were sick or of divers diseases, and cast out many devils; and suffered not the devils to speak, because they knew him.*

The summer of 2005, I was out west visiting my friends and planned on holding spiritual ceremonies together. In the mean time, an elder was out tending to his small farm, and I went along to see if I could be of any help. The lamb had maggots eating thru its one leg, and it didn't want to heal like the other lamb had done. I prayed on the lamb asking for God to heal the animal if it be his will in Jesus name. The next morning the lamb had a turnaround; all the maggots were dead and the flesh was healing.

The elder ask me to bless the animals and the farm if I could because it had been hit with devils. I said that I would see what I could do. The reason I don't make any promises is because it is not up to me. I'm just a tool for Jesus to work through. He does the healing; Jesus makes the decision on the fate of a demon. And they know him as the son of the highest God. Later that day, I went to walk by a calf, which seems normal physically, but a force got my attention. The animal was possessed with an unclean spirit. I commanded the unclean spirit out of the calf, but made a grave mistake in my view. The unclean spirit must be commanded where to go through the authority of Jesus Christ, and I didn't do that. So the unclean spirit went up the road and jumped into a little dog. The little dog could not bear this, so he went and lay under the wheel of a pickup that is always being moved. It wasn't even five minutes; I was informed of the little dog's fate.

Now, knowing what had happened, it was too late. There is nothing that I am permitted to do or undo. The elders then proceed to tell me that others are having problems with their farms, and they think that it is from demons. Later that day, one of the elders asked if my wife and I could go north to his ranch and do a blessing. The horses and jackass had been sick for some time, and no one could figure out why. Later that night my wife and I were on our way about a 400 mile trip.

The next day when we had arrived, everything looked normal as it usually will on the surface. The ranch was what you would expect it to be with some goats, dogs, and horses. The animals even looked good. A few had some sores, but nothing to get out of shape about. The elder said he can't get them to eat. And the small sores won't heal. I was standing on the front corner edge of the ranch; it was quiet, too quiet. I slowly started to walk into the field with my smough stick in my hand and my bag with chief stuff in it hanging around my neck. The bag was a gift from an Aztec Madison man. It is a hand-woven bag that they or a high priest would wear. I also had some holy water with me in a bottle. I had gotten it from a waterfall that the Madison men had used years ago. Then I had blessed the water; it was sweet water clan.

As I was walking past the horses, time was slowing down; that is good. This is what I need so that I can look into the spirit world. I can't tell you how to do this; it is a spiritual gift from the Creator. Now I can see past the physical world and maybe find out what the problem really is all about. As I was walking through this world, I pray with every step, sending my prayers to the Creator on smoke and asking for permission to see the unclean spirits that might be causing all the problems. I had seen it on the jackass first. It worried so much of its worth, something to do, that their mind was consumed with self worth, a value of work that there was no work. The jackass came down with a very bad depression, because she started to believe what the demon had told her; that she had no value; that she wasn't loved or needed. The animal was not eating, hoping to die.

These demons jumped from animal to animal spreading lies and deceit, robbing them of their will to live, thinking that they are not important, loved, or needed. This was the lie of the century. These animals were chosen for a very important job in the future. But the problem started when they, the horses and ass, weren't shown the truth. And this allowed the demons a great opportunity to undo their spirit. That's right, a lack of work attention value allowed their minds to go astray in some cases and broke their spirit; their will. I was granted the power through Christ to set things straight with some of them. And the ones that had their burdens and sins lifted from them were very grateful. They, the animals, showed this by following me around even though I was a stranger with no food and only burning sage and tobacco. Some, like the first jackass that had bad depression, came across the field and pushed her way through the other to thank me. The ass put its forehead to my forehead and just looked into my eyes. And I say to her, "Thank Christ for setting you free so not to die twice, but to live forever in God's grace."And if you think that animals don't go to heaven, you need to read your Bible some more. But unfortunately, the evil in the area wasn't going to stay away for long.

Spirit Animals

[2 Ki. 2:11 - 12; 6:13-17; Zech. 1:8-11; 6:1-8; Rom. 1:20; 2 Cor 12:1-4; Rev. 19:11-21]

Healing

In today's society, we have a pill for just about everything that you can think of and more. We have pills for things that are real, and things to meet the pill that are not real just so you think that they are. The truth is that a lot of these pills, in my opinion, are only to cover up or to relieve the symptoms and give you other problems, sometimes even causing a greater illness or death. If this is not good enough, then you are to go back in to see the pill pusher, oops, I mean Doctor.

Don't misunderstand me, most doctors mean well, but they are limited to their training and understanding of the human body, but not all sickness is physical. As a matter of fact, I think most of it is spiritual first, and then turns physical, or makes physical or mental problems. Not to say nothing is physical, but I

48

think we have it turned around for the most part. Some of sickness is from our surroundings and outside source, sometimes passed down through generation to generation. This can be physical or mental and/or come from spirit. I can and I will prove to you what I am saying.

Man is created in three parts, and all three parts must be addressed to truly be healed, not just made comfortable and always needing a pill or whatever it may be. If you are always in need of it, then you're not healed. Let's use AIDs or herpes, for example: I hear on the news and from people that their disease isn't curable, yet you can live longer if you take the pill or pills, and in some cases with fewer break outs. That really means you can live longer wrongly. I will explain.

What they are telling you is that as long as you keep living wrong, you need us, the pill pusher, the doctor, to keep living longer. They can't heal you. This is how you may get healed if it's not too late. Keep taking the medication, but stop the behavior that got you into trouble in the first place. Stop having sex out of marriage; no multiple partners; do not commit adultery; stop having sex with the same sex; no sex with animals or children. And don't have sex improperly {unnaturally} with your wife. If same sex fornication was meant to be, someone would have babies. This will be very hard to do and will take a lot of attempts at first, but when the thought or the urge comes over you, stop, stop everything. Sit down and think of something like your arm, then when it tries to pop up again, put the thought out of your head and start again. At first it will be a real tug of war, because it is a war you have turned over to your flesh and mind because of these choices you made before, and if you have a disease from it, you are in it deep.

The war is with the unclean spirit or spirits that you gave your mind to, and chose not to listen to your conscience; the Holy Ghost that can live within you, and guide you, if you wish. Then, after time and many attempts, you will be able to stand back and look at this thought that the unclean spirit has put into your mind, and do nothing with it; don't act on it or act it out, for you will lose. Ask the

Creator to help you, and give all of your heart to Him; don't just know Him; that won't work. You have to go all the way, and at first it may be scary and it will be painful. And don't think you can make a deal or go back to your old ways later. If you do, you will be in even more trouble yet. The only one that will make a deal with your mind and/or flesh is a demon. A lot of groups, and even churches, think that this is nonsense and want to change God's Word, and some people try and say that even Native Americans thought that it is ok. That is far from the truth. In the old days, Natives live by the laws of nature, not of man's mind. If it wasn't the way the animal lived, then it wasn't the way they lived, but this was thought to be primitive when the Europeans came. But it's not just the Europeans at fault. We didn't have to make some of the choices that we did. Sometimes the price of convinces is too great, for aids or herpes do not care what color your skin is. Now let's see what the Bible has to say about this before a special interest group has it removed.

Romans 1 Ch. 1

26   For this cause God gave them up unto vile affections: for even their women did change the natural use into that which is against nature:

27 And likewise also the man, leaving the natural use of the woman, burned in their Lust one toward another; men with men working that which is unseemly, and receiving in themselves that recompence of their error which was meet.

28 And even as they did not like to retain God in their knowledge, God gave them over to a reprobate mind, to do those things which are not convenient;

God lives in your heart if you let him; not in your mind. That can be given to unclean spirits which will then be allowed to have its way with the physical you. And it will eat you alive until there is nothing left. And then the real you, the spirit, may have no home and could die. So then you will get to die twice physically, and then perhaps spiritually. What a bargain for a short time of fun.

There are a lot of different ways to live out of the natural realm, and then you will likely come down with a sickness of the mind or of the body. Sometimes both. The root of the problem most of the time is spiritual, but no one today thinks this is true. This is 2006. As they say, get with the times. They are truly saying to be worldly; being neck deep in self indulgence is ok. If this is right and I am wrong, then why are there so many diseases that are far from a cure?

Here is a good one to try on. About six years ago, a young woman came to me and said, "Chief, I have a real problem." She said for years that she has been having seizures, and that the doctors can't help much, but to try and slow them down. The doctors couldn't fix the problem, and they didn't think that they ever could. She went on to say that they have gotten so bad that she probably would never be allowed to drive again even after she would be eligible after the D.W.I. was over.

Stop and think about this; she had some fun only to be condemned to a life of sickness, and of dependency. So I ask the young woman, "What do you want from me."

She replied, "Could you try and bless me? You know, smudge me." In the old days, a Sachem would smudge you with smoke and prayers to help clean you from the ugly spirits that may have come in contact with you and brushed into you in your daily life. Sometimes some of us will be allowed to even see what has happened because of such encounters. Let me tell you people, call it a gift, but it is almost always ugly; and even worse when you are only allowed to see, but not help.

So the next day we went up to a waterfall where our ancestors had done some fishing about 220 years ago. It was a nice, mild summer day, and I had brought with me my Chiefs stuff and a bag that a true medicine man had passed on to me with a few private things in side. As I start the smudge, I told the woman to truly pray and to be calm and still. In just a short time, I could feel the unclean spirit, quite a few of them, but the only one that I was given permission to see was in her head and neck. I could feel it like a big shield or block. So I went into deeper prayer, and finally the world came to a stop.

This is good. Nothing of this world matters now. I am in the spirit world on earth. Now I can truly see. At first it's blurry and bright. Sometimes, if dark, it takes a minute for my spirit eyes to focus.

Ok, now it's clear to me. This is what I have seen; a round, white mass with holes in it, and darkness in the holes, many of them. There was also a connecting stem that was similar. At first, I did not know what I was looking at. Then it had come to me. This was what was left of the woman's brain and brain stem. The woman had made such bad choices of behavior and had so much substance abuse, the bad spirit was embedded deep into her brain and brain stem. Now if this wasn't bad enough, it was consuming it and wasn't having any plans as when to stop. This spirit was going to kill the woman soon. So now there was only one thing that I could do.

I prayed for her soul to the Creator and for him to rid her of this demon. At the same time, I am running my left hand from the base of her neck up over the head, very slowly; without any firm physical contact all the way to the front center of the forehead.

Seeing that God had given permission for this, I was able to feel and see the process. It was a little hard on the woman. She had some tremors during the process. The Creator removed the spirit and stopped the advancing, but her brain and brain stem looked like spider webs. When it was over, the woman came around and almost fell to the ground, complaining of sightedness and a splitting headache. I said to her, "It will pass quickly," and it did. I didn't tell the woman what I had seen.

A year may have passed. She was free of the seizures. So when talking on the phone, I told her to talk to the doctor and see about coming off the drugs. From my understanding, she came off the pills and has been seizure free for a total of six years, but she has other battles to address as we all do.

Hell On Earth, Heaven From Above

This subject, believe it or not, has become an issue of debate, but more sadly today it's not talked about more than ten minutes. We spend more time talking about the neighbors and all their troubles, or what was on the TV last night. Let's take a look at some of the questions about Heaven and hell that you may have. Some people say that hell doesn't exist, or that hell is not a real place.

There is only one level of hell. You know this is just a metaphor; you can't take everything in the Bible to heart. Some ministers will tell you that when people in the Bible are describing hell, it is mostly figuratively so that you may understand. They will take things from another part of the Bible, and from a completely different subject that is clearly a metaphor of speech, and draw a parallel. Bull!! You bet your life hell is everything the Bible says that it is, and nothing less. No metaphor, and by no means, not a bit of the stretch of the imagination.

People say the men that wrote these things about heaven and hell are just men. Maybe so. But they were inspired by God through dreams, angels, and the Holy Ghost. They knew how to be still; something most of us don't know how to do. Jesus said, "Be still and know." What he is telling you is that you have all of the answers to your problems to these issues. It's in you. It's in all of us, the spirit. But, it must have you slow down sometimes to know. Some people are even having the same thought about heaven and whether or not it is a real place. Even more troubling, there are men and women of the cloth not telling you the truth, the whole truth, if you like, about heaven, with along hell. On a side note, women are not to be ministers, pastors, preachers, or rabbis, Chief, or sachem, or so on. These things are to be handled by men, not women.

1 Corinthians Ch. 11 vs. 3

But I would, you know, that the head of every man is Christ ;and the head of the woman is the man ; and the head of Christ is God.

In most cases, they have been misled and brainwashed over the years, as all of America has been; brainwashed and or misled on most of the important things in life. I am going to try and explain to you what I have learned about this subject the best that I can. I have also made a diagram to help you better understand what I am about to show you. To make it a little easier to understand, I have made a number system for marking each level. This is just a tool to use; a way to understand the order of things, nothing more. Let's start at the top and work our way down, no pun intended.

The 3rd Level of Heaven

The 3rd level of Heaven is the final place of heaven. You can't go any further or any higher. The 3rd level is north of the planet earth; it is higher than the clouds and higher than the stars. The 3rd level of Heaven is a physical place. It is a planet that is right. I said a planet. Let's look at what the bible has to say [King James].

Genesis Ch. 2 vs 1 *Thus the heavens and the earth were finished and all the host of them.*

This is the planet that God has his kingdom on now. There is a nation in heaven just like we have nations here on earth. On the planet heaven, God has animals just like the animals here on earth. There are also animals that are clearly different than the ones you see on earth. In the kingdom of heaven, the people are of perfect health. There are angels that live in heaven, and you will find that God really does have a throne to sit on. God has a spirit body. He, God, has his son Jesus sitting on his right. In the kingdom of heaven, God has twenty-four saints around him.

The city in heaven is clearly described in the Bible down to the measurements. So if there is anything different, I believe it is only because it is more than you can understand right now. So, yes I am saying the streets are paved in gold, and if anyone tells you different, all you have to say is, "Have you been there?"

All we truly know is that Jesus said that his father has many rooms prepared for us. The only way to find out is to find out for yourself.

And when Jesus comes to take you before his father and opens the book of life, hopefully, as Paul Harvey would say, "Now you know the rest of the story."

2nd Level of Heaven

This may get just a little confusing for some people, but please bear with me. You may have to read this chapter a few times, and, by all means, use your Bible. That is what it is for; to understand these gifts that are there for all of us.

Unlike the 3rd level of heaven that has only a spirit to its existence, the 2nd level of heaven has a physical side and a spiritual side to it. Please don't get up, let me show you. The physical side of the 2nd level of heaven you can just start to make out on a clear night. The stars that you look up at; that's, right, they are part of the 2nd level of heaven that you can see. The spiritual part that you cannot see is the angels that God has assigned to them. God, the Creator of all things, assigned some angels to stars and planets. I didn't make this up. It is in the Bible; Arch angels or Chief angels who rule kingdoms and planets.

1 Th. 4:16; Jude 9, Dan. 10:13, 21

Revelation Ch. 1. Vs. 20

The mystery of the seven stars which thou sawest in my right hand, and the seven golden Candlesticks. The seven stars are the angels of the seven churches: and the seven Candlesticks which thou sawest are the seven churches.

Some Native Americans have stories about the star people. Some tribes believe that they are the ancestors of the star people. In some families this very well may be true. Some of them say that the original star people were angels; beings greater than us; almost like gods themselves, and that the star people came to earth and made human beings to colonize the earth. Remember when Satan and the rebelling angels came to earth. The angles fornicated with the human women of this planet even though they were forbidden to do so.

Now, don't misunderstand me. Yes, sometimes you can see an angel, but not often, and only when they want you to. The true nature of an angel is in spirit with adaptations to the rules, but that is a whole book in its self.

1st Level of Heaven

The 1st level of heaven also has a physical side, along with a spiritual side. The physical side of the 1st level of heaven is just above the clouds here on earth. You are allowed to see this side of heaven, and even sometimes you may travel through this part of heaven in the physical body.

The Native Americans had always known this to be true. This is where you can get a taste of heaven. You can get up on a mountain top and have a better chance of having the Creator or spirits help you. The old native stories talk about the spirits dancing on the mountain tops. They also have stories about the spirits holding their meetings on the mountain tops. This is why the medicine men go up to the mountain tops to get answers. Also, this is why you will find the medicine wheels on a hill top. Also, if you get a chance to lie down in a medicine wheel, you can see planets and stars are aligned to this wheel.

Don't go in a medicine wheel without permission from council. This is a very sacred tool to the Native American and is not to be violated in any way. The Hopi Indians have stories about the kachinas that the spirits of the kachinas can sometimes be seen dancing on the mountain tops. And that is where the kachinas have their council meetings.

1st Level of Hell

This is the 1st level of hell right here on the planet earth. Back in the beginning, the earth was, I think, to be a heaven on earth, but with the tensions that arose in the kingdom of heaven, and then an all out rebellion between God and Satan with one third of the angels, the Creator assigned the planet earth to Satan along with the rebel angels.

Rebel Angels

Azazel, Semjaza, Armaros, Araklba, Baraqijal, Kokabel, Shamsiel, Rameel, Turel; this is the names of the Chief rebel angels, and you can find them in the book of Enoch. The rebel angels and Satan were still unsatisfied and were determined to pollute what God had created in his own image, man. The fallen angels could not have offspring amongst themselves, so they chose to commit the sin of fornication with the human women on earth and have children with them. This is out of the angel's natural realm, and it is a sin to do this. The outcome was a human that sometimes was

65

a giant. I call these people half breads. They have unnatural powers to both estates. These people are most likely stronger, smarter, faster, wealthy, men of power, and counting; the list goes on. This was an abomination to God. So the Creator destroyed the earth to rid it of the uncleanness. In the mean time, God had called Satan back up to heaven to explain himself.

Job Ch. 2 vs. 1-2

1 *Again there was a day when the sons of God came to present themselves before the Lord, and Satan came also among them to present himself before the Lord.*

2 *And the Lord said unto Satan, from whence comest thou? And Satan answered the Lord, and said, from going to and fro in the earth, and walking up and down in it.*

Also read **Job Ch. 1 vs. 7-8**

Satan was sent back down to earth to only repeat the unholy acts against God again. These angels, I think, were passing themselves off as Gods to the humans on earth. I think that the fallen angels went so far as to build the great pyramids and say that they are Gods, and that this was the kingdom of heaven. That is truly thumbing their noses to God. And this theory would explain a lot, like Greek mythology, not alone how and why the pyramids were built. Remember there was a time when man had no pain, nor death. He was like God himself in a lot of ways. But man, Adam, allowed his woman to seduce him, and all he had to do was say, "Eve, now put the fruit down. I love you, but the Creator comes first. And that is all that we need to know Eve."

So hell was allowed to continue on again thru women here on earth. How? We now have pain, and pain through child birth. Man can only live to around 120 years. Man was allowed to communicate with the animal and is now only to be afraid of him. Hell is now on earth through the mind of man from the unclean spirits that he allows, by his emotions that are unclean.

Read that last sentence again and again. It covers volumes of books. Right now, for the most part, the rule is that the unclean spirit needs you to physically operate in this world. Stop and think about it, they want to separate you from your Creator. How better to do this but to get you to act through your unchecked emotions. These are hate, anger, discontent, unnatural love, and the list goes on. In the 2nd level of hell you will see the way the unclean spirits have to operate this way. But remember, women cannot help but to bring hell on earth. It is an inherited sin passed down. They can only recognize it and control it.

It is man's job to love the hell out of a woman by putting God first and being firm with her, and loving. And for man to not love the hell in women. This will always be a battle, so remember to choose them wisely and always stand for what is right. Walk away when need be as to not get angry; only to return to the battle with a clear and loving heart, not weakness. And at the end of the day, you will have won the spiritual war, and your family will be better off for this. Anything less is not a man.

2nd Level of Hell

The 2nd level of hell is below the surface of the earth in total darkness. This place can't be seen by man normally, in the physical world on earth. The 2nd level of hell is the place that God had sent the fallen angel that I was talking about earlier. After the fallout over the fornication with human women on earth, God bound those angels on earth in chains to darkness. That means that these angels are not free to move around. They have nothing but total darkness. That means that these angels are no longer messengers of God, that they are separated from God. They will not live in the grace of God anymore, just pitch black darkness and powerless. These angels can't come to the surface to be amongst us. Also, they are not permitted into heaven anymore. They have lost their angelical powers. This is a devastating position to be put in.

You have to remember, just like you and me, they, the angels, chose to sin time and time again. This is sin by omission. There are western Native American Indians that have stories about the four levels of earth. If I remember right, they start in the center of the earth and work their way up through a hole on the surface to climb out from. The story goes into great detail.

Sometimes I think some people are able to see just a small piece of this hell. For example, when this happens, what a person might see is a very dark spot in the grass, almost black. Sometimes you may be driving at night, and you will see a very dark spot on the roadway like a big hole, and then it will start to grow. You may even see the dark hole make a tear in mid air. These could be port holes into the 2nd level of hell.

The 3rd Level of Hell

This is the big one. This is the hell that you hear about all of the time. In this level of hell, there is forever torment and pain beyond my abilities to explain. This is where you will find brimstone and fire; that is, if you want to.

In the 3rd level of hell, you are down deep below the earth. This is where countless numbers of condemned souls are to spend eternity. The 3rd level of hell is where you will die for a second time. On earth, you will die the first time of a physical death. Then, if you are sent to the 3rd level of hell, you get to die for a 2nd time. In that, you will die spiritually. I really don't know how to fully explain this to you. The only man that has ever come from the kingdom of heaven, then walked on earth and went all the way to the very pit of hell, and then back to his father again, and holds the keys to hell, is Jesus. Jesus is the only one; the son of God. Satan has been to all three places, but he is not in the form of man. Satan is a fallen angel; big difference.

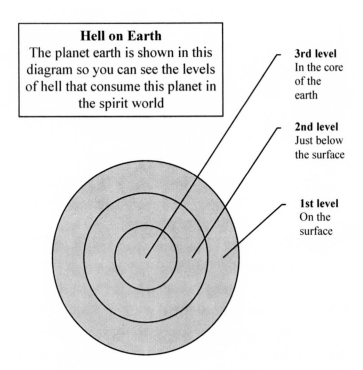

Hell on Earth
The planet earth is shown in this diagram so you can see the levels of hell that consume this planet in the spirit world

3rd level
In the core of the earth

2nd level
Just below the surface

1st level
On the surface

Heaven the kingdom. Physical place where God lives	**3rd**	3rd level of Heaven a planet, a spirit place.
God assigns angels to stars	**2nd**	2nd level of Heaven stars.
Man can see the transitional level of Heaven.	**1st**	1st level of Heaven is above the clouds.
God assigned this planet to satan.	**-1st**	1st level of hell on planet earth.
The fallen angels bound to darkness for moving out of their natural state.	**-2nd**	2nd level of hell. A spirit place just below the surface of the earth.
A place of eternal torment. The condemned die in this place daily.	**-3rd**	3rd level of hell. A place of brimstone and fire deep in the earth.

Shape Shifters

Over the years there has been a wide range of ideas on what shape shifters are and what they look like and can or can't do. A lot of the info about shape shifters has been greatly distorted to fit Hollywood's needs. They have made them into giants, animals, birds, witches, and mostly serial killers. Whatever will sell at the time, that is what it will become, thus making yet another joke out of the truth about Native American spiritual ways and making it easier to poke fun of. This pollutes and dilutes the truth. All this has done was to confuse, and mislead, the native communities and tear away at the soul of the people. When I have finished telling you what very little that I know about shape shifters, you may see how important this entity was in Native communities.

Physical or Not

Let's start with this case in point. Most people when they think of shape shifters, they think of a man or woman that has the magical power of physically changing into an animal or bird. That is the most common preconception that I know of that is out there.

The truth of the matter, in my limited experience, in such matter, is far from this. I have never seen a physical being, whether it of mankind or of animal kind, display the ability to shape shift in the spiritual state. This means that they could move out of the physical body, mostly when in a slumber or trans-like state. The trans-like state would be induced by many different means. One may go on a fast for many days and then take part in a ceremony like a sweat, or even a vision quest. Then as the soul would move from the body, the person could only then take the form of an animal or bird. This does have its limitations and provocations. Just keep in mind that the physical stays physical and the spiritual stays spiritual. But the spirit is the one that changes its shape, and again, this is so rare that even for the people that can see into the spirit world from time to time, it has become almost nonexistent. If you think you have seen the physical change, for example, a man disappears and in his place is a deer or a bird, get away. This should not be able to happen, and I would suspect witchcraft or demonic power involved. It's all one in the same; deceitful and wrong.

Who Were Shape Shifters

Shape shifters are not from the normal run of the mill man or woman. A person that has the ability to shape shift was most likely to be very spiritual and one with nature. To most people, this man or woman would not quite fit and had very strange ways about him or her. And most likely the person was of very high standing in the community, like a medicine man or a holy man, or both one in the same. Sometimes a shape shifter is misunderstood to the point that they become an outcast for many reasons, such as peace of mind on both ends; peace of mind for the community for fear because of ignorance; and for the shape shifter, peace of mind from all the precaution of being a witch; sometimes just to get away from so many people wanting the shape shifter to save the day at every turn. Keep in mind, not all chiefs, medicine men, and so on have this gift. It is very rare and almost unheard of today.

Why Shape Shift

There are many reasons for shape shifting, but it is mostly for flexibility to do what otherwise couldn't have been done. In most cases, it will be done to help the tribe in a bad position. For example, there may be no more food in the known hunting grounds, and the tribe won't make another winter without fresh meat and water. The young men themselves can't scout any further, so at council, the options are laid out, and then no one has any sound answers.

The Chief has decided to hold a sweat with the elders under the advice of the faith keeper. At the sweat, the matter at hand will be addressed. The men will each go on their spiritual journey in hope of a solution for their people's dilemma. Know that the man with the ability to shape shift has been put under the right conditions. He will allow his spirit to leave his physical body while under the protection of the sweat lodge. At this time, the spirit will shape from a man to an eagle. The eagle can fly high, fast, and far, with an eye out for the food and water so much needed. This is not the same as a spirit guide. A spirit guide is a separate spirit from your own. When the man can't go any more, or has found what he is looking for, the eagle will come back to the body of the man. The spirit eagle will turn into the spirit man and then go into the skin suit of the man. This information has been lost for so long that almost everyone will tell you that it is wrong, and you should say to them, "Show me."

The Little Dog That Could

I think it was back in the summer of 2000. I was in my tractor trailer pulling a long grade in Yakima. Luck is not on my side this day. "Bang," the sound snapped from under the hold. Then I lost power, and banging away, I went up the hill, echoing across the high desert like a John Deer Tractor, hoping that the truck would make it to the next town, wherever that might be, trying to not look up at my stack as to not confirm that I had dropped an injector or two; ah, yes, two. And that's how it all began.

I found a Kenworth dealer who was more than happy to inform me that I did lose two injectors. What this meant was: get a room and stick around for a day or two. In the process, it just so happened that the shop manager had some little Boston Terriers for sale. The next evening my truck was up and running, so I was going to stay the night and get going in the morning. I ran out with the shop manager to have a look at the puppies.

My miniature Schnauzer had to retire from the truck a year early. After seven years of the fast life, she had come down with full blown diabetes. I told her she needed to lay off the red man plug and beer.

Anyways, when we got to the house, I was outside as the manager retrieved the remaining pups from the feces-filled tub, to only put them in the yard with a piece of chicken wire set up in a circle. I had noticed that a big cat had been on the property within a few days. I asked the man about this, and he said, "Ah yeah, I only lost two pups." Then the eight-year-old boy was allowed to pick them up by the middle of the back and turn them over with its belly facing up as he swung around. That was it for me. I took the last seven hundred dollars to my name and gave three hundred fifty of it for the pup that came to me the most.

Within a few weeks I thought that there was something wrong with this dog. No matter what I did, she just would not respond. It got me thinking this dog was born on the reservation. Maybe I will try some Mohawk on her. Then she looked at me really stupid. Ok, now I am on to something. The next day I called some friends that spoke Laycota Sue. I got some words to try, and they worked within days. This dog was only able to learn native language. So I got my tapes out and brushed up on the old Mohawk with the puppy learning by my side. I also noticed that she loved to listen to western native songs. As time went on, I found that she loved to partake in all the Native American ceremonies. The little dog even loved to stand on her hind legs and take in a dance or two; this is no lie. I was accused of making the little dog learn all of this like a trick. The fact is that she, now at the age of one, was doing the ceremonies at will with others and insisting on it.

At this time I realized, whether she likes it or not, she must learn English for her own safety. This was hard for her to learn; a whole year of intense training and with a poor outcome. In the mean time, the little dog was now teaching me a few things like what plants were medicine or poison. Needless to say, I didn't catch on too well.

It gets even stranger. One night Missy, that's the little dog's name, and I was in Atlanta, Georgia. going for a walk up a dimly lit road as we often would do. On this night it all became clear. As we were walking, with the street lights on the left, I felt something. I looked around and didn't see anything or anyone, but just then, as I looked to the right of Missy, there it was; her shadow. But not just a shadow. It was changing. That's right, as we walked, the little dog's shadow was changing shapes. Missy's shadow was of a goat, then of a burro, then of a man. Missy acted like nothing was wrong. Then it would go in the reverse order.

This went on for a good quarter of a mile. It had taken me many attempts to find out in little bits and pieces what was going on with Missy.

One day in a sweat, I got most of the story about this little dog. A long time ago Missy was not a dog; she wasn't even a she. Missy was a very rare type of medicine man called a Hutta'lee. I know that is not how to spell this; just sound it out. Some say that they have been known to bring people back from the dead in a few cases. Needless to say, they, the Hutta'lee, is a very strong spiritual person. The Hutta'lee is not allowed to do any healing to advance his own agenda, or to take any money for his service. From what little that I could find out, Missy didn't heal someone when she should have, in order to advance her own interest. So later, Missy was given another chance to learn what she did was wrong, but had to live as a little dog and still help people. She could still shape shift, but always had to return to the flesh of a little dog. And I learned that she despised this with great resentment.

The winter of 2003, Missy and I were in Michigan, and an older couple had lost a Boston Terrier after nineteen years. I had never met the people before in my life, but somehow I knew that the man was with cancer and he didn't know, but Missy and I both knew. It was Christmas and cold, so Missy was wearing her little blue tee shirt. When outside, she had on her favorite coat. It too was blue and had a fur hood. Anyway, we were all inside, and I asked Missy, "Do you need to go with these people?" in native language. Missy got up and walked over to the man and climbed all over him. She never even looked back. I have never again seen or heard from her or them again; only to hear later that the man did get diagnosed too late, but somehow pulled through it, and that Missy was doing good. Some people that knew about Missy think that she could be an angel. It is true. Some angels look like animals to us, but I don't think this is the case.

Glowing Wheat

It was a fairly warm summer day in Spiceland, Indiana, on a Saturday. My wife and I were walking back from a sprint car race. Along the way back, we were walking on a dirt road against a field of weeds. Then it happened. "Hello. Over here. Here in the field." It was a very faint, soft, but clear voice. I stopped and looked. I saw nothing. Then I cleared my mind of all my thoughts and cares. He was in amongst all the weeds, but not to be choked out of sight; a small patch of wheat only to be seen as such by most. He said, "I heard your thoughts and prayers as you were walking. You know they are heard."

I replied, "Yes, but I wonder sometimes."

He, the wheat, said, "Tell her to look on me and you will be reminded. And she will see."

At this time, the wheat showed its spirit within. The most warm, lavender glow was starting to be radiated out from the wheat. At this time I had asked my wife if she could see. At first she could only see wheat. I said to her that she needs to try to clear her mind of all thoughts and her spirit. At first, nothing. The wheat was starting to glow more intensely. I said, "He, the Great Spirit, is in all things."

Then it happened. She said, "I can see it!"

"What can you see?"

She said, "I can see the sun glowing through the wheat. It's lavender; the sun makes it look nice," she said. At that time the wheat began to rustle, but the wind was not keeping pace. My wife did take notice of that and the fact that the color got brighter. In fact, the wheat became so bright that it almost overtook the wheat. As this was happening, I was saying to my wife to remember God is in all things. God can give us so much, but we have to have our hearts open.

A good example is in **Exodus Ch. 3 vs. 2**

- **2** *And the angle of the LORD appeared unto him in a flame of fire out of the midst of a bush: and he looked, and, behold, the bush burned with fire, and the bush was not consumed.*

Moses wasn't seeing things or misled. The bush was not burnt. If it would have been a geothermal gas fire, the bush would not last long. Yes, you can take the Bible for what it says to you. It is very clear if you are ready to learn and listen to all the lessons that are illustrated, and in most cases, if a verse is a metaphor, you are shown that it is. So we need to stop beating around the bush and face the truth, or miss out on so much.

The Twelve Spirits

It was around the end of June 2005 that I was to have another gift bestowed on me. I had a lot of new questions and concerns that I had been praying for answers most of the year. The more I study the Bible, the more I was concerned.

Finally, one night before going to bed, I had asked for guidance from the Creator and from my ancestors. At first I thought that I was having a dream, but it was much more. I was looking up into the heavens at the stars, as I so often do. After a short time, my attention was being drawn to a small group of distant stars. Nothing else mattered, just the stars. All of a sudden, I felt as if I was being suspended in space. I continued to look on the cluster of stars and think of all my questions. Then the stars started to come towards me at a steady pace, getting bigger and closer. Then, at once, they appeared right in front of me, twelve bright lights giving off a peaceful feeling.

The twelve lights began to take the shape of a person, but different. They were much taller than most people and had slender bodies and long faces. The beings didn't have any definition on their bodies. They didn't have any hair, no muscle, no clothes, not anything, but a glowing shape with eyes.

At the same time, I could feel the presence of another being, but I couldn't see it. And then the beings put me into an interactive vision. I am back on earth, and it is a nice sunny day. My wife and I are at a shopping center getting supplies. All of a sudden, rocks the size of your fist start to rain down from the sky like hell, causing a lot of damage to everything. The air was full of dust, making it hard to see across the parking lot.

We were having trouble finding our dually truck. A lot of people were hurt and disoriented, and there is a lot of collateral damage. If you didn't have a four wheel drive, you weren't going anywhere. My wife and I found the truck and had some people trying to take it from us, but we got into it and got away. My wife and I went to a hillside where we had found a cave. We made camp for the next few days. Outside the cave was a lot of fighting among the people for food and supplies; also, people from outside of this country at the same time.

Later, when things got quiet, in about three days, my wife and I went back into town for more supplies. It was hard to get around with dust-like dirt shin deep everywhere. As we were trying to finish where we had left off, my wife and I thought we would help some of the people. For the most part, we were unable to help. Most of the people wanted to fight you for everything that you had, and the others were just injured beyond help. My wife and I got two horses and two mules up to the cave. Then, shortly after that, we heard loud bangs of thunder and things slamming into other objects. I looked out from the cave; it was unreal. White, hot, glowing balls of fire were pounding everything. Nothing was left untouched; nothing.

This went on for a few hours. When it was over, it was very quiet outside. I waited a short time before going out of the cave to investigate. The earth was scorched for the most part; fires everywhere you looked. The pickup truck was of no use any more. I went back to the cave and got my wife. We rode the horses with the mules in town to see if anything was left. When trying to help some people, we came under small arms fire. We held our own and got them out of harms way. There wasn't many people left alive; my wife and I ran into small pockets of fighting.

Then, all of a sudden, I was back in space, standing in front of the twelve beings. I asked them, "Who are you, and what are you?"

They came very close to me and said, "We are your oldest ancestors. Remember at the sweat in September? We gave you warning of the event to come, but you only spoke of it to the people in the sweat. This time you must tell everyone, or you will be dealt with for not giving the warning, for you know this is to be true."

91

I could still feel the other's presence, but couldn't see him. Then, all at once the twelve spirits went back into the heavens in reverse, turning into stars again.

This visitation is biblically sound. I can explain. Saint John was shown revelation by an angel. Angels throughout the Bible are stars as they are seen fallen from the heavens. They are not to be mistaken; they should never be worshipped. You also must make sure of what type of angel you are confronted with. The definition of angel literally means messenger. A common angel is explained in **Ps. 104:4.** A common angel can look just like man found in **Gen. 18:2, 4, 8; Jug. 13:6; 1 Pet. 1:12; 1 Cor. 11:10.** *The first trumpet Hail fire, and blood rained from heaven.* **Revelation chapter 8, vs.7** *The first angel sounded, and there followed hail and fire mingled with blood, and they were cast upon the earth: and the third part of trees was burnt up, and all green grass was burnt up.*

The Mohawk Indians believe in beings sometime called star people. Some say that they are aliens; another race. In my view, they are spiritual bodies sent by the Creator to send messages to man. All one in the same, angels, aliens, but not the Creator, don't make that mistake and also make sure that it's not a fallen angel or demon. The Mormons believe that Native Americans are decedents of the twelve tribes of Israel. We are the Laminites that came from Liehi; the one who walked away from the light. Look it up.

Wakeup Call

On September 7, 2001, I was in Maine with family and friends visiting and having a Native American Sweat, as we have done in the past. There wasn't as large of a group this time, but it was good enough. My War Chief was there, along with a few men that were to be considered for Warriors. Some of the people were looking for answers; others healing; others for the experience.

I first began my day with the morning prayer to the Creator while greeting the sun and thanking the Creator for the sun. In my prayer, I gave thanks for all living things, small and big; things that crawl, walk, swim, and fly. I thank him for Mother Earth and all that she gives us that we take for granted every day. I thank him for the four winds, and the six directions, then I gave my offering of tobacco in all six directions.

After the prayer is completed, I then walk into a dance clockwise around the area that the lodge is to be. As I dance with a drum or rattle in hand, I am giving a blessing. In this case, I used a rattle. Now the sweat lodge can be set up. First, the Fire Keeper puts down wood in four directions, forming a cross, and then he will put down the kindling. On top of this he will lay some grandfathers stones. The Fire Keeper will then alternate wood and grandfathers until he is satisfied.

The Fire Keeper is in charge of many things. On this day, he will maintain the fire and keep the grandfathers hot. The Fire Keeper will also use deer antlers on short poles to move the grandfathers into the lodge as they are needed for each door. A door is a segment, or restart, after a pause of the sweat. There are commonly four of these doors. As most of the people are inside, The Fire Keeper may attend to any outside needs, but must keep the fire first. The stones, grandfathers, are to be gathered by the children eleven and under. They can't use sandstone or river rock.

The women should build the sweat lodge. We use young willow limbs and sticks. I like to have two poles about two inches around at the base, bent into an arch, with each end in the ground. I have the other poles cross over at the pick of the arch and put each end into the ground. Each end should face a magnetic direction. Tie the poles together on top where they meet with raw hide or twine. You need to have, from top to bottom, smaller sticks horizontal with the ground. Don't forget to leave a three foot door facing the east. Everything is tied with raw hide or twine. I like to keep my lodge about five to six feet at its highest point and have twenty-eight ribs, sticks, and limbs in total. Then, a hole needs to be dug into the ground in the center of the lodge big enough to hold at least eighteen grandfathers the size of your fist. Some people like to put tobacco ties inside, hanging from the top.

Now the lodge can be covered with animal hides and blankets, making it as dark as possible, leaving a flap for a door. Just outside of the door to the right, as you look at it from the outside, put the dirt from the hole in to a small mound. In the center of the mound, stick a stick with a father tied to it. This is where people will leave things of this world like rings and eye glasses before going into the lodge.

From the door east, make a walkway with a thin line of stones on each side of the door. The people must fast for one to three days before the sweat. After the sweat, there will be fruits to eat; strawberries are a must. And then later that evening, you will have a feast together. In our sweat, the women went in first, always going clock wise, then the Chief, and finally, the men. This way, the women sat on the side of the man's heart, and the chief and a woman would be just inside the door. The Chief or faith keeper or pipe keeper may run the sweat in my family.

There is a lot more that goes into a sweat and there are many different kinds of sweats, and different ways of doing them. This is to just give you a general idea of how it was done.

The people can have turns introducing themselves, asking for prayer, and take turns praying. This is done mostly when the sweat is in the 1st door. They can tell some jokes and stories if needed. The leader will let you know what is ok or not ok. There will then be some hot grandfathers brought in to the lodge; into the hole in the center of the lodge. I like to start with six; one for every direction. They are glowing hot, and if you listen, you may hear them moaning. Then, I like to put some tobacco and sage on them. Just a pinch of each and it should flame up into the air and then leave only smoke.

In the mean time, I leave the door open. After the pipe keeper, who I have sitting on my right, hands me the pipe in the proper way, I will give my prayer and pass the pipe around to everyone in the lodge to have a turn or to pass. When the pipe is returned to the pipe keeper, and he or she has separated the bowl from the steam, the pipe keeper will then empty the remaining contents into the grandfathers. Then I will have the fire keeper close the door. There is a pail inside with a wooden ladle and water. I then throw some water onto the grandfathers. This will make them hiss and sing as they are steaming and glowing. At this time it will get quiet for a short time. Then the door may be opened after things have slowed down. The people will have a few minutes to leave if they feel that they can't go on. Then more grandfathers are brought into the lodge. I like to have three more added to each door. Then the door is closed, and after a few seconds, the water is added.

This is repeated until you have completed four doors. In this sweat, I was given a vision that I didn't fully understand at the time. In the third door, it had gotten very dark. Then it started to snow just a little. I never saw snow in a lodge before. Everyone was seeing this at the same time. Then it started to get very hot, and the snow turned to rain. This is seen now and then rain inside a hot sweat lodge; it is a welcome.

Finally, after the weather had settled down, so had the people inside. I then went into deep prayer. The outside world didn't matter anymore. It just slows to a stop and then disappears. There is no sound, no odor; there is nothing. You can even see time stop. Then, bam, I am standing on the ground looking up, not knowing why. I can't make out much. All I see are two tall objects standing close to each other. The sky is smoke-filled and ash is falling. I thought it was two mountains, one being volcanic. As I am moving around trying to get a better view, I saw something hit the second mountain out of the corner of my eye. All I can see now is flames and ash coming down so heavy that it became a white out.

Instantly, I found myself seeing the Pentagon hit with what I believed to be a missile. There was again so much smoke it was hard to make out much of anything. People were covered in soot and blood, running around in disbelief. Then I see an explosion in the sky in another location and something plowing into the hill side at a high rate of speed. It was so fast that I wasn't able to make heads or tells out of anything. Then it was gone in a flash. At the time all this is transpiring, I got the sense that all the events had happened on the eastern side of the United States and within minutes of each other. I also was lead to believe that it was a deliberate attack. So I assumed a missile attack on the United States. I saw a fifth explosion somewhere on the west coast in a wide open area. It looked like a big tire Mack. This was a flash and it was gone, but I do know it also came from the sky. I was confused of how could this happen so fast and with no warning.

Then I asked the Creator for some help to understand what has just been shown to me. Out of the dark, a small group of glowing beings came forward. They are very tall and thin; so bright that I couldn't make out anything but their outline. I asked them, "Who are you, and what are you?"

One of them said, "We were sent to help. You must tell everyone what you have just seen: five attacks simultaneous on the United States of America." Then the glowing beings faded away as they moved away. I came back into this world very tired. After a few minutes setting quietly, I told the people in the lodge that the United States will be attacked from the air five times. I think it is done with missiles, not nukes, but almost as bad. They will come out of nowhere, with no warning.

As you can imagine, all kinds of questions came my way that I had no answers for. This was the end of the third door; everyone was finished. I stayed for the fourth and final door. The last door came up empty for me. As you know, on September 11, 2001, the United States was attacked by an invisible enemy. Three of the five were able to complete what they had set out to do. We must never forget. And yes, this is a spiritual war, and it is very much real.

Stone People

It was a nice and moderately warm day in Idaho. My wife and I were on a combined vacation and business trip into the middle of nowhere. You could be safe to say 100 miles from nowhere in any direction. We had the camper set up for a few days in a canyon.

On a friend's land, just getting to camp was a small adventure in itself. We had to cross several canyons and a mountain range. The last canyon's bridge was almost in a shoe horn

Chief James R. Sherbaugh, Jr.

and narrow. Thank God no one was coming the other way. Our rig is fifty-four feet long and has ten wheels. At more than one point we were nose to tail, only inches from the walls of the bridge and always in a curve. The view was breathtaking, that is if you are not the one driving. The easy part was going down into the canyon where we would stay the night or two.

I thought I would never say this, but the automatic Allison transmission made child's play of the steep downgrades. Just lock out the overdrive and put the tow mode on, and the truck did all the work on its own and brought us down safely to the bottom. That evening, we sat up the trailer with the river to our back, and the hot spring from above rushing into the river. The hot springs were about 128 degrees to 168 degrees, at any given time. This water had been used by the Native Americans for hundreds of years. The hot spring water was not your normal hot spring of the area. It has been said to be a fountain of youth by the Natives and the local white communities.

I know this first hand, that the water can sit in a clear plastic drinking bottle for a year, in uncontrolled temperatures and light, and in a year's time still have no smell, and taste as good as the day it was drawn. I also have taken the water to the E.P.A. testing lab in Ohio after the water was eight months old and had been in the drinking bottle. I subjected it to 106 degrees Fahrenheit and as low as 38 degrees Fahrenheit; also, light and darkness. The E.P.A. was left to believe that the water tested was under thirty hours old and was drawn from the ground into their testing jars. The test came back with no bacteria 24/24. The water also has the same P.H. levels as that of the human body. All I know is that it is the perfect water to this day, and when you sit in the water it draws the toxic out of you. I could actually feel it. This is definitely a special place.

The next day, when I was crossing the river below to get to the spring water, it happened; time slowed down; down to a crawl. As I looked up to the far bank just below the hot spring, I saw it. Or I should say I saw them; a small band of tribal people standing on the bank. The ages ran from toddlers to elders. The people were startled that I could see them. This hasn't happened, I guess, in some time; that is, that someone was able to see them. The Chief looked at me with kindness in his eyes. The two warriors were another story, but the Chief somehow knew the answer to all their concerns and told them that it was ok. I had found out that these people were the sweet water clan, and that the water is also their bother. And I have to tell you, if you didn't drink the water, it has a slight and mild sweet taste that goes away as quick as it came.

That night you could hear the red wolves singing to each other from the mountain tops. The temperature was in the mid eighties, and that was more than welcomed after 102 earlier that day. The next morning, the wife and I decided that we needed to head south, deeper into the canyon to a trading post near the Nevada state line. We dropped the travel trailer, and that wasn't really good enough. The trip was long, windy, and slow. The pickup truck was too heavy for the trail and sometimes too wide. We really should have been told to take a mule or a horse, but it all worked out. When my wife and I got into the heart of the canyon, we were given the most beautiful gift. And it begins like this.

My wife and I had gotten out of the truck to take some photos with the digital camera. As we started walking, my wife kept asking me if I felt it. I said, "No, I don't feel anything. It's nice and peaceful for once." She was persistent in asking me again, and I said, "No! It's nothing."

Then she said, "Do you see it? Do you see it? It's following me."

I said, "No. What? I don't see anything." By this time she was getting annoyed, and I think a little shaken. I said to her, "I can't see anything out of the normal, but that doesn't mean that it is not there. So what do you see?"

She said, "An eye."

I said, "Ok, where?"

She points to a big rock in the side of the mountain, at the back, only a few feet away.

She said, "You can't see it?" And then she started to move around to see if the eye is there or moving with her.

"Woman, what are you doing?" I said.

My wife said, "See, it is following my every move."

I said, "Ok, I can't see it so let's move on."

In the meantime, my wife is feeling that we are being watched. Come to find out, she may have been right all along. As we went around the next bend, the rocks were very unusual, and so was the feeling. As I looked up at the large protruding formation of rocks out of the side of the hill, I started to see shapes of people. I looked away and back again, and there it was, as clear as day, people; stone people; frozen in time on the side of the hill, and I am not talking just about outlines of people. These stone people were in great detail. As a matter of fact, if they were in any greater detail, you would have thought that someone took the time to carve them out of the hillside. But I assure you that this was not the case. It was with no doubt this was a good sized Native American tribe. In their period clothing, they stood there bigger than life itself. A woman was holding a baby, and men standing all around. They were proudly wearing their feathers, and somehow, at the same time, very sad.

Then, just a few more yards, my wife and I came upon another group of stone people. These people were in a much tighter group. This was a group of men only, all facing the eastern sun. The men were dressed very nice; as a matter of fact, you could not help but notice how nice the head dresses were and the decorative clothing that the man displayed. These men were chiefs, but for some reason, there was a lot of chiefs standing around looking on to the east with great power and respect; but at the same time, with sadness in their hearts, so it seemed.

By the way, my wife was given the same gift to see all of these things. And surprisingly, we were given permission to take some photos. After a few moments in amusement, we pushed forward. My wife and I had only to travel a few 100 yards, and we were shown even more. As we got closer to a large crop of free-standing rocks from the ground, we could see a figure of a man with his back to us. The man had on a long robe and a bonnet or hat of some type. His hands were together in front of him. This man was facing another group of rocks that looked like a pile of wood with a man laying on it. The man on the wood was facing up, lying on his back. His head was near the standing man. Right about now, you are saying to yourself, *I am crazy.* But before you do, take a look for yourself. In real life, the photos are even more revealing.

There is a story around all of this. You see, God and spirit talk to us in many different ways, but we just seem to be too busy to notice, even at the most pro known messages. The stone people were real at one time. This was an event that had taken place years ago. The eye that my wife first felt and then saw was a warrior scout. He was at the corner, looking over, to give his people warning if trouble came near. This is the stone face on the book jacket. If you look, you will see a tear just below the eye. The people had come north from Nevada looking for the water that was said to heal the sick. On the way, their Chief had died, and this is where you see he was being prayed over, and being prepared for cremation. The other chiefs were there to give condolence to the Chief that passed on. I would have said this was a powerful and respected man because of how many other chiefs had come to show their respect, but that wasn't the case. This chief was loved by the weak and the small; great and strong; the young and the old. This was, and is, truly a great chief. The saddest part of it all is that the people had to go only a half day more even with women and children to get to the water. The water that they traveled so far for.

Fornication Of A Great Nation

The United States of America is the greatest nation on the face of the earth, but the American people are letting it slip away, and fast. Let me explain. It is your responsibility to keep this nation great, by keeping it in God's grace and laws. It is true this is the land of milk and honey, but you must remember that if you take milk and honey out of the jar, you must also put something back, or the jar will go empty. Also, if you don't keep the lid on the honey, it will get contaminated, and the milk will sour.

Yes, that is right. I am addressing the immigration issue. There needs to be a lid on it, and the laws need to be followed and enforced. If you can't do this, the country will be destroyed. This goes for everyone, and the American people can't always sit back and take out of the jar without putting anything in.

Someone has to do the work to have the fruits. Milk and honey don't drip out of the thin air. Also remember that every time you vote for an entitlement from the government, chances are that you will also vote away another part of your constitutional right or even an inhalable right from God.

What I am about to say now is also just as important as the other subjects are. They intertwine to each other. There is not one federal government official; not one that is your savior. Not one of them should have anything to do with your personal life. The only major role of the federal government should be to uphold the constitution of the United States of America under God for which it stands.

What I am about to say is a general statement about the behavior of the nation as a whole with some exceptions of humanity, so hold on. The truth is about to pier us, you, and it might hurt. The United States of America is under an attack from all sides inside and out. This attack has started from spirit and has now manifested into the physical world. The government that we think we have is not looking out for the nation's best interest under God. The American people are not looking out for anything in the long run. They, the American people, have been brainwashed and broken in so many ways it is so complicated, but yet so simple. It goes like this. Nations are used to carry out the objectives of God and Satan in the physical world, sometimes just as individuals are also used. The United States is a noble nation but is losing its nobility as we speak. I believe that there are about three hundred very powerful and rich men {bankers}, some of which are in the Federal Reserve. By the way, it is not a branch of the United States government. These men are globalists, and their love of money and power is stronger than their love of God. How do I know this? It is overwhelmingly obvious because of their actions that speak louder than words. It is like the wind. It may not be seen, but the effects on the world are very real.

I also believe that these men are in control of our government and other governments. They are the puppet masters. Now I am going to show you what should be obvious to you, but isn't. You need to slow down, and do not react out of emotion, and look back and then forward. The family unit has been deliberately dismantled over the last forty years. The wife now has to leave the home to help sustain the income and taxes. In doing so, it opens your family to more brainwashing. I mean influence. As you are at work outside of the home, the school and school programs, and sometimes government, have a great hold on your child. And then when you and your spouse are at home with your children, you're sometimes not really there. Your body is there, but your mind and spirit are not. And from the time that a child is born, until about the age of five years of age, this is detrimental to their development of the mind, spirit, and body. This is a planned attack by the men that I have spoke of earlier, the globalist; the ones that control our once noble nation.

Another attack is on our inalienable rights. This is being executed by large, special interest groups that are lobbying congress. And their goal is to remove God from this Nation, and it is a win-win for Congress so they think, because the government gets more money and power over you. What's not to love [God], now that so many of you handed over your parental rights to the government through many different venues, willing and unwillingly.

There are proponents of the government that have said, and continue to say, that even the Mention of God and/or Jesus in any government influenced institution will not be tolerated, but alternative life styles such as homosexuals and lesbians and premarital sex are not only embraced; it is taught. I thought schools are to be using the tax dollars to teach reading, writing, and math. The only thing they are teaching with any real success is how to live longer wrongly! So you can teach perversion and bring Satan into the children's lives, but don't dare bring God and/or Christ into the mix! This is the objective: suppress the conscience and embrace the now; the feel good.

This allows you and your children to become subjects of the government and/or the one-world order, and to also help pay out the money at the same time. As you are given a trinket from Uncle Sam, you grow to want more and more for less. Now that God is spoken of less and less, it is sometimes almost a crime to even talk about God. But you are ok with that over time, and some of you so-called Christians will even defend that God should only have a certain time and place.

But, the alternative life style is allowed everywhere and any time. Now that you have been stripped of your conscience and only have false elusions of God, you have a void and a need; a hunger to fill that void. You will fill it by eating more, buying more toys, and thinking that you need more material things that you can't afford. But, you are in the frame of mind that you deserve more things, and that, if it feels good, no matter what the result, you do it or get it. So now you get sick from an infliction and you need help.

The spirit has been allowed to go through the motions only at best, and for only a fraction of the day one day a week. But the ungodly is allowed to consume you, all day and every day. And you are given mental and physical warnings and a conscience warning, if you still have one, but you squelch it out. Then you put God on the back burner, and your animal wants and needs on the fast track.

Finally, the pain from your life becomes so great that the good spirit is kept away and sometimes even never allowed to return. So now you have even allowed your mind to become as sick as your body, and the pain, physical or mental, is so great that you are out of control, and then you run to the doctor or the dealer for a pill that will suppress the pain or the systems, which, in a lot of cases, the government controls one way or another. And the three hundred men that lean on the government make money on an artificial comforter that is not ever going to heal you, but only to have you needing more and more. So you spend more money and become dependent on it. You should get a doctor's help, but don't stop there. You should also allow God to help your spirit so that you can get to the root of the problem. Ask him, God, back into your heart, and don't just go through the motions. Take action by making changes in your life, from unclean behavior to Godly ones. For example, stop overeating, drinking, and sex with anyone at any time, even in your mind. Start living for the future as to live forever, so that you may be reborn of the spirit, and you can live forever, not for the moment.

Living for the near future or the moment is one in the same. You are only allowing others, on and of this world, to have more control over you, and you will never be held. You may live longer wrong. This will allow you to pay more taxes and have less time for yourself and your family and God. All that, and you will have to buy more pills and/or alcohol, making everyone more money while bankrupting you spiritually and physically until you die. So, now that you have allowed yourself to be owned from the cradle to the grave and past the grave, you will be taxed one last time, and you have sold your soul in most cases, and have worked hard to do it. What a shame. It is over for you, and it's dark. There is nothing left to take or to give. *Our Father which art in heaven, hallowed be they name. Thy kingdom come thy will be done on earth, as it is in heaven. Give us this day our daily bread. And forgive us our debts, as we forgive our debtors and lead us not into temptation, but deliver us from evil for thine is the kingdom. And the power, and the glory, forever Amen.*

Glossary

Angels: They are angelic beings created by God and used as messengers by God. They are the sons of God and have super natural powers.

Clan Mothers: Clan Mothers are the backbone of the tribe. They are the keepers of the headdress [the Chiefs]. They help guide his decisions. He must base them on seven generations ahead. It is said a Clan mother must have 14 skins. She is the base of the family she represents. All things go through her. And she brings them to the Clan Chief if she needs to. A Clan Mother must follow the Great Law. Clan Mothers are to be chosen wisely; the title is for life with little to no exception.

Demons: Unclean spirits that are ruled by Satan and know God's plan for man. They can go in and out of man or animal at will if permitted to. They are individuals and smart.

False Face Society: This is an accent secret society from the five nations in the north eastern part of North America. Now the Six Nations, the men are usually prominent men of the tribe and are medicine men and Chiefs. Every spring they send a runner out to let the people know they are coming, so that the people can open their homes to them. The men are wearing ceremonial clothes and mask. The mask is shaped like a deformed crazy face of a person or a demon. This mask is doing two things: scarring off evil spirits and hiding the man's identity. The mask is carved out of a live tree, then is painted and has horse hair on top and/or corn silk. There is a set that the face or mask is made entirely of corn, after the men raid your house of evil spirits from the winter past. Then you give them a gift, but not money, and then they move to the next house.

Fornication: This is a spiritual word to describe a blaspheme against God through the act of a sexual encounter that is not natural to the parties involved. This is against God's will. Here are some examples: when some of the angels that came to earth and mated with human females, when a man is on man or a women on women, or when a man or a woman has committed adultery or has sex with children or animals.

Grand Father: In the north eastern Native American Indian, there are three types of Grand Fathers.

1. The Chiefs of a Grand council or your clan chief when at home.
2. Your father's father is a grandfather unless a Chief is in the room, then he is respectfully called old man.
3. The stones or rocks from the earth that are believed by Native Americans to be the oldest and wisest. They are the blood and bones of your ancestors. They will sing to you when used properly in the sweat lodge.

Kacheenas: There are three types of kacheenas.

1. The man, he must be at least 12 years old and he dances in ceremonies wearing a mask to hide his identity. The man emulates the spirit he is masquerading to be. This man is usually a holy man for the people, or trying to become a priest. This custom comes from the Western North American Indian.

2. **Dolls:** Different families have different dolls. The dolls are played with by children and are a learning tool for them; sometimes to teach the children about good and evil.

3. **Spirit:** These are good and evil spirits that work behind the physical world of the western people. There are many types. You may see them where they live on top of a mountain dancing on a lake in the mist.

Natural Estate: This is a spiritual word meaning that a man can conduct him or herself in the grace of God and within the laws of The Ten Commandments.

Sachem: This is a native word for Chief that sometimes is also a spiritual type of Chief with God-given powers. He always puts the peoples' interest first by making his choices seven generations ahead, and not because of one person's gain. The whole of the people comes first. So he operates in this manner. How will it affect the people seven generations from now? How will it affect the people now? How will it affect the individual? His services are not to be bought with money. You should give him gifts like food, clothes, tobacco, and lodging. Sachem should be chosen wisely by following the Great Law, because he is for life and is very hard to remove from office.

Shape Shifters: A spirit that comes from a man or women and has the power to transform into an animal or bird. This allows the person to be in two places at one time if they need to, and allows them to take advantage of the new shapes and natural powers, like flying or running fast.

Skin Walkers: Witches that used bones from a baby, or today, a cow. The bones are ground into a small pellet or ball and then used to deliver spells. These are ungodly men.

Printed in the United States
205782BV00001B/223-288/P

9 781598 249378